D0297909

Sch

00 400 960 926

HEADLINE ISSUES

Feeding
the
World

Sarah Levete

www.heinemannlibrary.co.uk
Visit our website to find out more information about **Heinemann Library** books.

To order:
☎ Phone 44 (0) 1865 888066
▤ Send a fax to 44 (0) 1865 314091
▢ Visit the Heinemann Bookshop at www.heinemannlibrary.co.uk to browse our catalogue and order online.

Heinemann Library is an imprint of Capstone Global Library Limited, a company incorporated in England and Wales having its registered office at 7 Pilgrim Street, London, EC4V 6LB - Registered company number: 6695582

"Heinemann" is a registered trademark of Pearson Education Limited, under licence to Capstone Global Library Limited

Text © Capstone Global Library Limited 2009
First published in hardback in 2009
The moral rights of the proprietor have been asserted.

All rights reserved. No part of this publication may be reproduced in any form or by any means (including photocopying or storing it in any medium by electronic means and whether or not transiently or incidentally to some other use of this publication) without the written permission of the copyright owner, except in accordance with the provisions of the Copyright, Designs and Patents Act 1988 or under the terms of a licence issued by the Copyright Licensing Agency, Saffron House, 6-10 Kirby Street, London EC1N 8TS (www.cla.co.uk). Applications for the copyright owner's written permission should be addressed to the publisher.

Edited by Sarah Eason and Leon Gray
Designed by Calcium and Rob Norridge
Original illustrations © Capstone Global Library Limited 2009
Illustrated by Geoff Ward
Picture research by Maria Joannou
Originated by Heinemann Library
Printed and bound in China by CTPS

ISBN 978 0 431162 72 0 (hardback)
13 12 11 10 09
10 9 8 7 6 5 4 3 2 1

British Library Cataloguing in Publication Data
Levete, Sarah
  Feeding the world. - (Headline issues)
  1. Food supply - Juvenile literature 2. Malnutrition
  - Juvenile literature
  I. Title
  363.8
A full catalogue record for this book is available from the British Library.

Acknowledgements
We would like to thank the following for permission to reproduce photographs:
Corbis: 13r, Peter Adams 15b, 22–23, Khaled El Fiqi/EPA 24, Ronnie Kaufman 28, Jehad Nga 25, Caroline Penn 8, José Fuste Raga/Zefa 20, Wendy Stone 21; Istockphoto: Greg Gardner 12, Paul Velgos 23; PA Photos: DPA Deutsche Press-Agentur 27l; Rex Features: Sipa Press 17; Shutterstock: 5r, 7b, 8, 10, 14, 16, 24, 26, 12, Vera Bogaerts 18–19, 19, Murray Gilmour Breingan 11, Pablo H Caridad 18, Devi 1, 6–7, Anna Dzondzua 13l, EcoPrint 14–15, 15t, Anton Foltin 9, Hannamariah 4, Sia Chen How 6–7, Khoo Si Lin 27r, 27, Steve Mann 16, Ilja Ma ík 4–5, 5, Dmitry Rukhlenko 3, 7t, Carolina K. Smith, M.D 11, Maree Stachel-Williamson 22–23c, Michaela Steininger 10; Still Pictures: Joerg Boethling 29, 30–31.

Cover photograph reproduced with permission of Corbis/Adrian Arbib.

Every effort has been made to contact copyright holders of material reproduced in this book. Any omissions will be rectified in subsequent printings if notice is given to the publishers.

Disclaimer
All the Internet addresses (URLs) given in this book were valid at the time of going to press. However, due to the dynamic nature of the Internet, some addresses may have changed, or sites may have changed or ceased to exist since publication. While the author and Publishers regret any inconvenience this may cause readers, no responsibility for any such changes can be accepted by either the author or the Publishers.

Northamptonshire Libraries & Information Service	
00 400 960 926	
Peters	06-May-2009
363.8	£12.50

Contents

Some words are printed in bold, **like this**. You can find out what they mean by looking in the glossary on page 30.

Investigating food

D ID YOU EAT school dinners or take lunch in with you today? You and your friends probably had lots of different foods to eat. How is your food produced and how does it get from a farm to your lunch box? Many children do not have enough to eat in some parts of the world. Can planet Earth provide enough food to feed all of the people in the world?

People need to eat a range of foods to stay healthy. They include carbohydrates, proteins, vitamins, minerals, and fats.

Why we need food

Food provides people with **nutrients**. Nutrients are the good parts of food that provide the body with energy. Different cells in the human body need energy to do their different jobs. Muscle cells use energy to move the body. Nerve cells use energy to send messages around the body. Bone cells use energy to support the body. Nutrients also help the body to grow and stay healthy.

A varied diet

Different types of food provide different nutrients. Carbohydrates are a good source of energy. Foods with plenty of carbohydrates include potatoes and cereals, such as corn, oats, rice, and wheat. Protein helps the body's muscles, bones, and other organs grow and stay healthy. Beans, dairy products (milk and food made from milk, such as cheese and yoghurt), fish, meat, and nuts are packed with protein. Dairy products also provide fats. These give the body lots of energy for growth. Fruits and vegetables are full of vitamins and minerals, which help keep the body healthy.

BEHIND THE HEADLINES
Hunt or farm?

About four million years ago, prehistoric people were **hunter-gatherers**. They roamed the countryside looking for animals to kill and searching for plants and berries to eat. About 12,000 years ago, people started to plant seeds to grow food. Groups of people settled around lakes and rivers, where the crops grew best. They kept animals for meat and milk. Farming had begun. Since then, new technologies have transformed the way people produce food. Today, there are only a few communities of hunter-gatherers left in very remote parts of the world.

Machines such as tractors have made the job of farming the land much easier than before.

Farming for food

MUCH OF THE food people eat comes from a farm – even the food in packets or tins. Growing plants or keeping animals and selling or using them for food is called **agriculture**.

Crops and livestock

Crop farmers grow plants for food. These include grains such as **maize**, rice, and wheat as well as fruits and vegetables such as apples, carrots, and potatoes. Livestock farmers keep animals such as cows for meat and milk and chickens for meat and eggs.

Land and weather

The landscape is all the different features in an area. It includes deep valleys, tall mountains, and crowded cities. The climate is the average weather conditions in a particular area. Both the landscape and climate influence what type of plants can grow in any region.

Living off the land

Cows need plenty of space in which to roam and graze. They live in open fields in **continents** as far apart as Australasia and the Americas. With their shaggy coats and padded feet, llamas and mountain goats are more suited to crossing narrow passes in cold mountainous areas.

Farming basics

Crops grow in the **soil**. Plants grow best in **fertile** soil. Fertile soil is moist and full of nutrients or goodness. There are different types of soil in different parts of the world. The type of soil depends on the climate and the landscape. The type of soil affects the plants and animals that can live in the area. Some wetlands have very damp soil. Mangrove trees grow well in wetlands. By contrast, the soil is dry and dusty in the desert. Cacti grow well in the deserts.

FACT!
- 41 per cent of all the grain grown in the world is maize.
- The United States produces 40 per cent of the world's maize.
- 70 per cent of the maize produced worldwide is fed to livestock.

ON THE SPOT
Indonesia

In the flat parts of Indonesia, farmers plant rice seeds in **paddy fields**. Low walls surround the paddy fields so the farmer can flood them. As the rice seeds grow, their roots suck up nutrients from the water. In hilly areas where there is less water to flood the fields, farmers grow a different type of rice. They plant it in fields cut into the hills like steps. This rice seed takes up nutrients from the soil.

Where the land is hilly, farmers cut steps into the slopes so they can grow rice.

Tundra
Coniferous forest
Broadleaf forest
Grassland
Savannah
Semi-desert
Desert
Subtropical forest
Monsoon forest
Tropical rainforest

This map shows the different types of natural vegetation in the world.

World water crisis

WITHOUT WATER, THERE is no life. Plants on a windowsill or flowers in the garden die without enough water. People need water to survive, too. We drink it to quench our thirst. Farmers need it to grow the crops that people eat. Farmers also need water for their livestock. Like people and plants, animals need to drink water, too.

These Ethiopian women are carrying jugs of water on their heads. They have collected the water from Lake Tana.

Drink up

In 2008, the world population was 6.6 billion. People are using more water than ever. Millions of people still do not have clean drinking water. In some **developing countries**, women and children walk for many miles every day to fill up buckets and jugs from a river or a well. This water is not always safe to drink. Every year, millions of people die from diseases caused by drinking unclean water.

Water for farms

In areas where the **soil** is very dry, farmers need water to **irrigate** their land. Irrigation involves diverting water from lakes and rivers and using it to help crops grow.

Irrigation wastes about 55 per cent of the water taken from lakes and rivers. The water either trickles away through the soil or evaporates (dries up) in the hot air before it reaches the crops. There must be a better way to water the crops.

FACT!

✦ People in rich countries use ten times more water than people in the developing world.

✦ A person could live for a month without food but would die within a week without water.

✦ Most people who do not have clean water live in the developing world.

ON THE SPOT
Colorado River

The Colorado River in the United States cuts through 2,320 kilometres (1,450 miles) of mountains and deserts. It supplies fresh water to 25 million people and water to more than 3 million acres (1.2 million hectares) of farmland. Where the Colorado River meets the sea, the river has nearly dried up. The area around it is no longer full of life. It is just sun-baked mud.

Wyoming

Nevada   Utah

Colorado

Colorado River

Arizona   New
Mexico

Mexico

Very little water from the Colorado River now reaches the sea. Much of the water has been **diverted** (forced to flow a different direction) to irrigate the crops grown in California.

Food or fuel – time to choose

Do you EAT fish, meat, or vegetables? Do you like all three? What type of fuel do your parents use to fill up the car? The food people choose to eat affects what is available for others to eat. The fuels people use for energy also affect the lives of others.

Cows eat about 8 kilograms (17.5 pounds) of grain or meal for 1 kilogram (2.2 pounds) of beef they produce.

Meat or veg?

Today, people eat more meat than they used to. Farmers raise more livestock to meet the demand. Cows graze on grass. The farmer also feeds the cows grain. Farming livestock takes up more space than growing crops such as rice and wheat. Many people think that the land should be used to grow crops. They believe that the grain fed to farm animals should be used to feed people instead.

Biofuels

People are concerned about **climate change**. Using **fossil fuels** such as coal, natural gas, and oil produces a **greenhouse gas** called carbon dioxide (CO_2). Too much CO_2 in the air leads to **global warming**. Today some people use **biofuels** instead of fossil fuels. Biofuels are made from plants such as rapeseed, sugar cane, and wheat.

FACT!
- ✦ There are three and a half times more livestock than people in the world.
- ✦ Farm animals use up 70 per cent of farmland.
- ✦ Farm animals eat one-third of the world's grain.

People should start using biofuels: Who is right and who is wrong?

FOR

Like fossil fuels, biofuels release CO_2 when they burn. The plants that make biofuels absorb lots of CO_2 when they grow. This makes biofuels more environmentally friendly than fossil fuels. Biofuels are also renewable. They won't run out because the crops from which they are made can be grown time and time again.

A driver fills up a car with biofuel. Food prices may be rising as more land is set aside to grow crops to make biofuels.

AGAINST

Growing plants for biofuels has led to a global food crisis. Farmers should use their land to grow crops to feed people, not grow plants for biofuels. The price of food is rising because more farmers are growing plants for biofuels. As a result, many people in poor countries are starving. If people want to make a difference, they should take a bus or the train instead of driving their cars. Governments should also invest in clean energy sources such as solar and wind power.

Is organic the answer?

INSECTS, DISEASE, AND poor **soil**... all of these things can destroy a farmer's crop. Since farming began on a large scale, farmers have tried to increase the amount of food they produce and to ensure that their crops are not damaged.

Make food

Many farmers spray their crops with chemicals. Some chemicals, called **pesticides**, stop insects from damaging the crops. Others, called **fertilizers,** make the soil more **fertile**. This helps the crops grow bigger more quickly. This type of farming is called **intensive farming**. It helps the farmer to grow lots of food very quickly.

Animals can also be farmed intensively. They live in cramped conditions. Some chickens are kept in cages. The cages are so small that the chickens can barely move. Farmers often use chemicals to make them grow more quickly. Then they are killed for their meat.

Look after the land

Some farmers do not like using chemicals. **Sustainable farming** means looking after the soil naturally. Farmers use manure (animal droppings) to make the soil fertile. **Organic farming** is one type of sustainable farming. Organic farming takes longer to produce food, so it is more expensive.

A farmer sprays a field with chemicals to kill any insects that would damage the crops.

People should buy organic foods: Who is right and who is wrong?

Many people believe that chemicals damage the long-term health of the soil. They think that animals should not be fed with chemicals. Chemicals also **seep** into rivers and lakes, polluting the water supply.

FOR

"I spend more on organic produce because I don't want my children to eat food that is full of chemicals. We've got to think of the future of the land. Who knows what all the chemicals have done to the soil? What are they doing to the food we eat?"

Organic farming (left) involves a lot more work than intensive farming (right) and so organic produce is much more expensive.

AGAINST

"I can't afford to buy organic food. I can't afford to worry about chemicals or the future of the soil. I just need enough to feed my family."

Taking too much – are we overfarming?

FARMERS ARE OFTEN keen to produce as much food as possible. However, overfarming the **soil** can ruin it. It destroys the fertility of the soil and makes the land useless for future farming.

Overgrazing

If livestock remain on a piece of land for too long, they overgraze. They eat all the grass, which doesn't have a chance to grow back properly. As they trample on the ground, the livestock compact the soil. This makes it harder for other plants to grow.

Fish feeding fish!

Fish are an important source of protein. People are eating more and more fish. To keep up with the demand, some farmers run fish "farms". Farmed fish are usually fed with fishmeal, which is made partly from wild fish.

It takes 3 tonnes (3.3 tons) of wild fish to make enough fishmeal to feed 1 tonne (0.9 tons) of farmed salmon. However, the 3 tonnes of wild fish could be used to feed people instead.

Just enough

In some parts of the developing world, farmers only grow enough food to feed their family. This is called **subsistence farming**. Since these farmers do not store food, they run the risk of having nothing to eat if there is a natural disaster or a poor harvest due to bad weather.

When crops fail, farmers often leave their families and travel to the city to look for work. The farmers send all the money they earn back to their families. They are left with very little money for themselves. Many live in poverty, with no home and no money to buy any food.

FACT!

✦ Fish numbers in the north Atlantic Ocean are just one-sixth of what they were 100 years ago.

✦ Unless we stop overfishing, by 2048 very few of the types of fish we eat today will be left in the oceans.

ON THE SPOT
Mozambique

The shallow waters off the coast of Mozambique used to teem with fish. Today, the local fishermen and women are despairing because they hardly catch any fish. There are very few fish left in the sea. The people who fish here cannot even catch enough fish to feed their families.

Fishermen and women from Mozambique pull an empty fishing net from the water.

According to one fisherman: "The large ships catch huge amounts of fish such as shrimps and tilapia. They catch too many fish too quickly so the stocks are running out."

Farmers often travel to cities to look for work when they cannot grow food to feed their families.

World climate in crisis

Our PLANET IS warming up. The ice caps are melting. Extreme weather events such as **hurricanes** and floods are more common. These changes to weather patterns are known as **climate change**.

Towering trees help to absorb CO_2 and release fresh oxygen into the air. This helps to control global warming. As forests are cleared to create land for farming, there are fewer trees to soak up the CO_2.

Climate change

Climate change has a major effect on the quantity and quality of food that farmers can grow. Scientists think that climate change is caused by too much carbon dioxide (CO_2) in the air. CO_2 is needed to trap some of the Sun's heat around the Earth. However, human activities, such as burning **fossil fuels** and clearing forests for farmland, are increasing the amount of CO_2 in the air. The temperature of the Earth is getting too hot. This is known as **global warming**.

Insect alert

Warmer weather means that some pests, such as aphids, start to hatch earlier each year. This presents problems for farmers as they try to deal with the increase in pests. Dark swarms of insects called locusts destroy crops. Warmer weather makes this more likely.

FACT!

By 2100 worldwide temperatures will have risen between 1.4°C (2.3°F) and 5.8°C (9.3°F). This will lead to climate change causing:
- ✦ more droughts (long periods without rain), causing crops to fail
- ✦ more land erosion because of the rising sea level
- ✦ more floods because of heavy rainfall

ON THE SPOT Myanmar

In May 2008, a massive storm called a cyclone swept through the country of Myanmar in South-east Asia. The cyclone battered everything in its path, killing tens of thousands of people. During the cyclone, fierce waves crashed over the land. The salty seawater destroyed the crops. Many people in Myanmar are facing starvation. Scientists cannot say for sure that climate change is responsible for severe weather events such as this cyclone. However, many people think that the increase in extreme weather events such as cyclones, droughts, and floods are linked to climate change.

Severe weather events such as cyclones destroy crops, livestock, and fishing equipment. People face poverty and starvation.

Disappearing land!

THERE IS A blustery wind and heavy rainfall on farms across the United States. The top layer of **soil**, called the topsoil, is rich in **nutrients**, but it washes away. This wearing away of the soil is part of a natural process called **erosion**.

People are speeding up the process of erosion. Trees and shrubs act as natural windbreaks and prevent the wind from blowing away the topsoil. However, **logging** companies and farmers are clearing huge areas of forest for timber and to grow crops. This makes the soil much more vulnerable to erosion.

Dusty, dry, and dead

Deserts are dry places with little plant life. People live on the edges of deserts. They chop down trees for firewood. Without trees, there is little to stop the wind from blowing away the topsoil. The deserts are spreading all over the world. There is less land for farming.

Houses or food?

More and more land is being used to build houses. Many people think that it should be kept for growing crops. They argue that there is little point in having a home if you cannot feed your family.

Once-rich farmland could become desert in the future because of logging.

FACT!

✦ It takes between 200 and 1,000 years to form 2.5 cm (1 inch) of fertile topsoil. Farmers lose this amount every 16 years – that's at least 12 times faster than it can be replaced.

BEHIND THE HEADLINES
Sea alert

As temperatures rise, ice caps in the north and south polar regions melt. Sea levels rise and flood land that could be used to grow crops. Scientists believe that rising sea levels could threaten the food supply of at least 200 million people.

Melting ice caps could be a serious threat to people living in coastal areas.

Food on the move

Have a look at the labels on the food in your fridge at home. Is the food locally produced or is it from another country, or even another **continent**? Much of the food eaten in **developed countries** is grown thousands of miles away. Sending food from one country to another creates huge amounts of pollution. This adds to the problem of **global warming**.

Not so "green" beans

A farmer grows green beans in the sunny climate of Kenya in Africa. She sells the beans to a supermarket chain in Britain. First, a lorry transports the beans from her farm to a factory. There, the beans are washed and wrapped in packaging. The beans are put into huge refrigerators and flown to London. Lorries pick up the beans from the airport and transport them to supermarkets around Britain. The beans are sold in the supermarket, thousands of miles from where they were actually grown.

Animals on the move

It's not just green beans that travel thousands of miles. Animals such as horses, pigs, and sheep are packed into lorries, too. Disease spreads quickly in the cramped lorries. After hours of travelling, the animals are slaughtered.

Pigs are transported on a crowded lorry. Many suffer horribly in the heat of the cramped conditions.

FACT! ✦ In July 2007, 85 pigs died from heat exhaustion on the way from Canada to Hawaii.

People should buy food from overseas: Who is right and who is wrong?

FOR

Growing green beans in Britain creates as much pollution as importing the beans from Kenya. A British farmer uses huge machines to harvest the beans. These machines run on fossil fuels and create lots of pollution. Buying beans from the Kenyan farmer keeps many people in Kenya in employment.

Green beans are taken for granted in Britain, but they may have travelled thousands of miles to end up on the dinner plate.

AGAINST

Importing green beans from Kenya creates a vast amount of pollution. Why not eat food produced locally and in season? This would help employ British farmers. The green beans grown in Kenya should be sold to local people or neighbouring countries.

Feast or famine?

One in seven people in the developing world does not eat enough food to lead a healthy lifestyle.

Source: The World Food Programme

In the developed world, one in ten children over six is overweight.

Source: International Obesity Task Force

HUNGER IS A BIG problem for many people in **developing countries**. People do not go to the shops to buy their food. When crops fail, many people face starvation. Hunger is not a problem for most people in the developed world. However, **obesity** (being severely overweight) is a problem. People eat too much in some parts of the world; in others, people starve.

Not enough to eat?

Television news reports often show the physical effects of hunger and starvation. Children who do not get enough **nutrients** from food are said to be **malnourished**. They are thin and frail, and their bodies are not strong enough to fight off diseases.

Hidden effects

There are many other hidden effects caused by not having enough food to eat. Hungry children miss school because they are more likely to become ill. If they do go to school, they may be so hungry that they cannot concentrate, which affects their ability to learn. A pregnant woman who does not have enough food cannot produce enough milk to feed her baby – and the baby is then hungry from the very moment he or she is born.

FACT!

✦ In 2006, around 854 million people faced starvation – that's more than the combined population of North America and the European Union.

✦ About 820 million of these people lived in the developing world.

BEHIND THE HEADLINES

Interview with a nutritionist

"Why are more and more people obese?"

"People like to eat foods packed with sugars and fats, and they do not take enough exercise. People travel by car instead of walking; machines do lots of work instead of people doing it. Children spend too much time playing computer games or watching television instead of playing sport."

What are the effects of being obese?
"Obese people often feel unhappy about themselves. As adults, they are likely to have conditions such as heart disease and high blood pressure."

Eating too much fatty food such as fried chicken and chips will contribute to obesity.

Key
■	+35%
■	20–34%
■	5–19%
■	2.5–4%
■	0–2.4%
□	No data

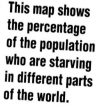

This map shows the percentage of the population who are starving in different parts of the world.

Why can't we feed the world?

AT THE MOMENT, the world makes enough food for everyone to eat. Why then are millions of people still dying from starvation? Poverty is the answer. Many people are so poor they cannot afford to buy food, even if it is available. The problems caused by **climate change** mean that crops are failing more than ever before. This is disastrous for the farmers who depend on what they grow to feed their families.

Many farmers grow "cash crops" such as coffee to make money. They sell or export the crops to the **developed countries**. Cash crops grow on land that could be used to grow food for the local people.

Stop press... June 2008

A worldwide food crisis took place in 2008. The price of food doubled in just one year. In countries such as Egypt, Haiti, and the Philippines, people could not afford to buy cereal grains such as corn, rice, and wheat. People started to riot.

The crisis was partly due to the land given up to grow plants for **biofuels**. It is partly due to the increased demand for meat. Much more farmland is set aside for grazing livestock than it is for growing crops. It was also partly due to the effect of climate change, which causes extreme weather events that are ruining the crops.

Protesters riot in response to food shortages in Egypt in 2008.

FACT!
✦ Six million children under the age of five die every year as a result of hunger.
✦ Every five seconds a child dies from the effects of starvation.

ON THE SPOT
Sudan

Women prepare a meal in a refugee camp in the Darfur region of Sudan. Many people face starvation in these camps.

In times of war or conflict, many people face starvation. Farmers are forced to flee their land. In the Darfur region of Sudan in Africa, different groups have been at war for several years. They are fighting over the rights to water and **fertile** land, as well as other problems. Millions of people had to leave their homes, land, and livelihood. They now live in refugee camps. In the camps, organizations such as Oxfam and Save the Children give out basic foods such as flour, oil, and sugar. However, many thousands of people, especially women and children, are still dying from starvation.

Tomorrow's news

WHAT DOES THE future hold in store for farming and food? The world's population is increasing very quickly. In 2008, the world population was 6.6 billion. By the year 2050, the population will have grown to more than 9 billion.

Farmers of tomorrow

The climate is also changing. How will the farmers of the future cope? Will they be able to produce enough to feed the growing population? Is the future in **organic farming** or will farmers turn to science to help them grow more crops?

Frankenstein or future?

Modern advances in technology allow scientists to mix different species or types of plant and animals. This is called **genetic modification** (GM).

GM crops are designed to resist certain diseases, to survive floods, or to grow with little water. Many people have concerns about the effect of GM crops on other plants.

They also look at the possible negative effects on the people who eat the crops.

At the moment, GM crops are not grown in Britain. In the United States, some potatoes, soy beans, and tomatoes have been grown using GM techniques. Many farmers in the developing world are growing GM crops. They do not care about the possible problems with GM crops. All they want is enough food to feed their starving people. Is it right to stop the farmers from doing so?

Soil-less

Hydroponics is a way of growing plants without using soil. The same **nutrients** that are present in soil are put in water and fed directly to the roots of the crops. Hydroponics uses less water than plants grown in the soil, and it takes up less space. Could this be the answer to the problems of climate change and an increasing population that needs feeding?

ON THE SPOT
Svalbard

On the remote islands of Svalbard near the icy North Pole, there is a giant underground building in which millions of seeds are being stored.

The store includes seeds from almost every type of crop. If a natural disaster wipes out any crops, the seeds will survive. Farming will continue and people will be fed.

Young seedlings grow at a hydroponics farm.

Sweetcorn was one of the first GM foods to be approved by the European Union.

Get involved!

EVERYONE SHOULD HAVE the right to eat healthy food, but this is not always the case. What farmers produce on their farms, what foods people choose to eat, and how people use energy makes a big difference to everyone on the Earth.

Try to follow some of these simple steps. It will help make a difference to the future of our planet.

People need to make responsible decisions about the food they choose to eat.

THINGS TO DO

A farmer from Tanzania collects cotton that will be made into Fairtrade clothing.

Eat well

- Eat plenty of fresh fruit and vegetables. They are healthier than pre-packed foods or foods that have been processed (had lots of things added to them).

Grow your own

- Buy a packet of seeds and grow your own vegetables. You don't need a huge garden or outdoor space – a flowerpot will do.

Food of the world

- Ask your teachers to set up links with schools in other countries. Find out about what other children eat. Plan some healthy menus that include different styles of cooking from around the world.

Save energy

- Are there ways you can reduce the amount of energy you use? Could you walk or cycle to school instead of getting a lift in the car?

Shopping

- Support local farmers by buying locally produced foods. Look at information on the packaging. Where does the food come from? How far has it travelled before arriving at the supermarket?

Fairtrade

- Think about buying **Fairtrade** produce. The farmer then has enough money to buy food for his or her family and will be able to afford medicine and clean water.

Glossary

agriculture farming the land to produce food for people

biofuel fuel made from plants such as corn and sugar cane

climate change unexpected changes to the weather caused by global warming

coniferous describing a plant or group of plants that bear cones

continent huge area of land usually surrounded by water. There are seven continents in the world.

developed country rich country

developing country poor country

diverted moved away from its normal course

erosion wearing away of the land

fertile able to support healthy plant growth

fertilizer substance put on soil to make it more fertile

fossil fuel fuel such as oil, coal, and gas. These fuels formed from the remains of plants and animals.

genetically modified (GM) food food made by mixing up features of animals and plants so they resist diseases or grow in a particular way

global warming increase in the average temperature at Earth's surface

greenhouse gas gas that traps the Sun's heat around the Earth

hunter-gatherer person who hunts animals and searches for food

hurricane severe storm that begins in the Atlantic Ocean or eastern Pacific Ocean

intensive farming farming on a huge scale, using chemicals

irrigate take water from rivers and lakes through a system of pipes and channels to water the land

logging cutting down trees for wood

maize cereal grain also known as corn

malnourished lacking enough food to keep the body healthy

monsoon seasonal wind that brings heavy rain and flooding

nutrient substance full of goodness or nourishment for healthy growth

obesity being very overweight

organic farming type of sustainable farming that does not use artificial fertilizers or pesticides

paddy field water-filled fields in which rice is grown

pesticide chemical sprayed on crops to kill insect pests

savannah grassland scattered with trees

seep slowly leak out of something

semi-desert area neighbouring a desert and another type of land

soil earth that plants grow in. It is made up of air, water, bits of gravel, and dead matter such as plant and animal remains and droppings.

subsistence farming growing only as much food as the farmer needs

subtropical area or climate that is nearly tropical

sustainable farming farming using natural substances and practices

tropical from part of the Earth near or on the Equator

tundra swampy land in the Arctic region that is frozen in winter

Find out more

Books

Feeding the World (First Starts), Janine Amos (Franklin Watts, 2002)

Food and Agriculture: How We Use the Land (Geography Focus), Louise Spilsbury (Raintree, 2007)

Food and the World (Your Environment), Julia Allen and Margaret Iggulden (Franklin Watts, 2008)

Food for All (Action for the Environment), Rufus Bellamy (Franklin Watts, 2006)

Food for Life (Sustainable Futures), John Baines (Smart Apple Media, 2006)

Websites

The World Food Programme website has lots of information about the global food crisis and what you can do to help: **www.wfp.org/**

The website of the Food and Agriculture Organization highlights global issues in the fight against hunger: **www.fao.org/**

This website is run by the charity Planet 21. It looks at some of the key issues that face the world, such as famine, health, and poverty, and tells you what you can do to help: **www.peopleandplanet.net/**

The website of Farming and Countryside Education (FACE) looks at food and sustainable farming: **www.face-online.org.uk/**

Index